LIFE IN A
ROMAN
FORT

JANE SHUTER

First published in Great Britain by Heinemann
Library, Halley Court, Jordan Hill, Oxford
OX2 8EJ, part of Harcourt Education.
Heinemann is a registered trademark of Harcourt
Education Ltd.

Produced for Heinemann Library by
    Bender Richardson White
Editor: Lionel Bender, Nancy Dickmann, Tanvi Rai
Designer and Media Conversion: Ben White and
    Ron Kamen
Illustrations: James Field, John James and
    Mark Bergin
Maps: Stefan Chabluk
Picture Researcher: Cathy Stastny and
    Maria Joannou
Production Controller: Kim Richardson and
    Séverine Ribierre

Originated by Ambassador Litho Ltd
Printed in China

ISBN 0 431 112983 (hardback)
09 08 07 06 05
10 9 8 7 6 5 4 3 2 1

ISBN 0 431 113068 (paperback)
10 09 08 07 06
10 9 8 7 6 5 4 3 2 1

British Library Cataloguing in Publication Data
Shuter, Jane
    Life in a Roman fort. - (Picture the past)
    355.1'0937
A full catalogue record for this book is available
from the British Library.

Acknowledgements:
The publishers would like to thank the following for
permission to reproduce photographs: Ancient
Art and Architecture/R. Sheridan pp. **6**, **8**, **10**, **14**,
15, **16**, **21**; Corbis Images Inc./Archivo
Iconografico, S. A. p. **7**; Corbis Images Inc./Jason
Hawkes p. **30**; David Cuzick /Visual Image p. **11**;
Duncan Gilbert p. **18**; Terry Griffiths/Magnet
Harlequin pp. **9**, **19**, **20**, **24**, **25**, **26**; Vindolanda
Trust pp. **22**, **23**, **28**; Werner Forman Archive p. **12**.

Cover photograph of Trajan's column
reproduced with permission of Ancient Art and
Architecture/R. Sheridan.

Any words appearing in bold, **like this**, are
explained in the Glossary.

www.heinemann.co.uk/library
Visit our website to find out more information
about **Heinemann Library** books.

To order:
☎ Phone 44 (0) 1865 888066
🖹 Send a fax to 44 (0) 1865 314091
💻 Visit the Heinemann Bookshop at
    www.heinemann.co.uk/library to browse our
    catalogue and order online.

ABOUT THIS BOOK

This book is about daily life in **forts**
in Roman times. The Romans ruled
from about 753 BC to AD 476. At
first, they ruled only the city of Rome,
in Italy, and the land around it.
However, they built a huge **empire**
by taking over more and more land
and ruling it with Roman **laws**. By
about AD 117 the Roman Empire was
huge. The Romans could not have
captured lands without their army.
They needed many soldiers and forts
to maintain the empire. Many local
people were unhappy with Roman
rule, and the army had to keep them
under control.

We have illustrated this book with
photographs of objects and forts from
Roman times. We have also used
artists' ideas of fort life. These
drawings are based on Roman forts
that have been found and
investigated by **archaeologists**.

The author

Jane Shuter is a professional writer and
editor of non-fiction books for children.
She graduated from Lancaster University in
1976 with a BA honours degree and then
earned a teaching qualification. She taught
from 1976 to 1983, changing to editing and
writing when her son was born. She lives in
Oxford with her husband and son.

Contents

Roman forts

The Roman army built an **empire** of captured lands for Rome from 753 BC. The Romans were not always welcome in the lands they took over. The army had to keep local people from taking back their lands. Its soldiers built a network of roads and **forts** to keep control of the empire. The army moved around to wherever trouble broke out. This was most likely in the places furthest from Rome, at the edges of the empire. In these places, Roman soldiers set up forts to protect its lands all year round.

Look for these:
The fort shows you the subject of each double-page chapter in the book. The soldier's helmet shows you boxes with interesting facts, figures and quotes about Roman forts.

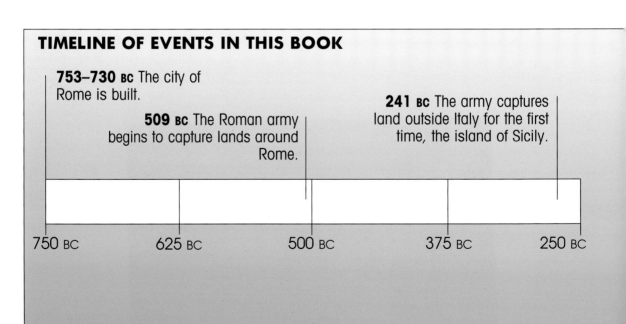

TIMELINE OF EVENTS IN THIS BOOK

753–730 BC The city of Rome is built.

509 BC The Roman army begins to capture lands around Rome.

241 BC The army captures land outside Italy for the first time, the island of Sicily.

750 BC 625 BC 500 BC 375 BC 250 BC

The Roman Empire
in AD 117

~ roads
☐ forts

North Sea

Britain

Rhine River

Germany

Danube River

ASIA

Atlantic Ocean

Black Sea

N

Rome Italy

Mediterranean Sea

AFRICA

0   500 miles
0   500 kilometres

Egypt

Nile River

Red Sea

This map shows the Roman Empire at its biggest, in about AD 117. The lines show the main roads. There were many more roads than this. The dots show the biggest forts on the edges of the empire.

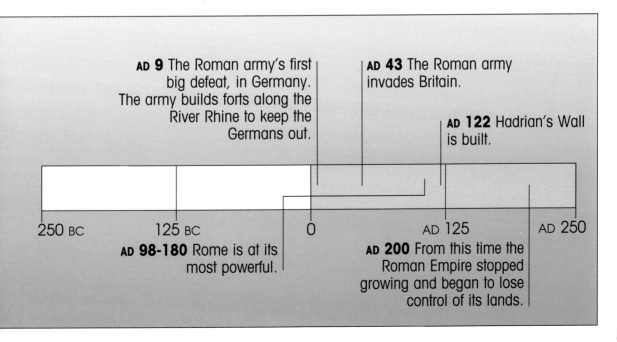

AD 9 The Roman army's first big defeat, in Germany. The army builds forts along the River Rhine to keep the Germans out.

AD 43 The Roman army invades Britain.

AD 122 Hadrian's Wall is built.

250 BC   125 BC   0   AD 125   AD 250

AD 98-180 Rome is at its most powerful.

AD 200 From this time the Roman Empire stopped growing and began to lose control of its lands.

The Roman army

The Roman army was very well organized. People who joined the army were put into groups of a hundred (a century) led by a **centurion**. Of the 100 men in a century, 80 were soldiers. The other 20 people kept the **records**, or had other skills the army needed – some were doctors, for example. Six centuries made up a **cohort**. Ten cohorts made a **legion**.

Soldiers trained to fight as a group. They practised making this *testudo* (tortoise-shaped) defence with their shields (below left), time and time again. When they had to do it in battle, they could do it very quickly.

Roman soldiers had to be able to do everything for themselves. They were not just fighters. They had to be able to make a safe camp quickly every night and feed themselves there. They had to build more permanent **forts** in lands they took over – and roads to link these new lands to the **empire**.

IN THE ARMY NOW

As the Roman Empire grew, it needed a full-time army. This was made up of:
- Roman citizens who chose to join the army
- people from countries taken over by Rome who volunteered
- captives from wars who were made to join.

Roman soldiers moved around the empire by sea as well as by road. This carving shows soldiers on a ship.

The edge of empire

As the Roman **Empire** grew, soldiers had to live further and further away from Rome. Britain was the furthest north the Romans went. Hadrian's Wall, built for the Roman emperor Hadrian, was begun in AD 122. It was finished in about AD 135. The wall marked the northern edge of the empire. It had **forts** along it and could only be crossed at guarded crossing places known as milecastles.

Hadrian's Wall was not built all at once, from one side to the other. It was built in sections. When it was finished, it stretched 117 km (73 miles), from one side of Britain to the other. It had sixteen forts spaced out along its length.

Soldiers came to the forts on Hadrian's Wall from all over the empire. Many came from northern Europe – modern-day Germany and Belgium. The Roman army did have British soldiers, but they were sent to other countries, not kept in Britain. The **praetor**, the commander in charge of the fort, was usually a Roman citizen, because the Romans did not completely trust local people.

On Hadrian's Wall in Britain, each **legion** built about 8 kilometres (5 miles) of wall. Some stones along the wall were carved to say which legion, or part of a legion, built that section.

LETTERS HOME

Over 300 Roman documents were found at Vindolanda Fort on Hadrian's Wall. Some list **stores**, others are letters. One letter to an ordinary soldier says: 'I have sent you some socks, two pairs of sandals and two pairs of underpants.'

Building the fort

When Roman soldiers first captured an area of land, they built a temporary **fort** from the poles they carried. Then they built permanent forts, with walls and deep ditches either side for safety. Forts were often built as part of a long defensive wall. If so, the wall also had smaller forts, called milecastles, dotted along them.

This famous Roman carving, called Trajan's Column, showed soldiers doing building work as well as fighting. Each **legion** had an **engineer**. He made sure that the forts were built properly.

The soldiers sometimes used local people to dig up and carry the stone for forts and walls, but they did most of the building work themselves. Forts were the same all over the **empire**. The headquarters, where the weapons and money were kept, was always in the middle of the fort, facing the main entrance.

In this fort, in the foreground there are barracks for soldiers. The headquarters are in the centre with a hospital and storehouse on the left, and the praetor's quarters and other officers on the right. At the back there are workshops and stables for the horses.

FORT FEATURES

Forts were often on a long defensive wall. They each had:
- a headquarters
- a house for the **praetor** in charge and his family
- **barracks** for the soldiers. Most forts held 800–1000 soldiers.
- a toilet block
- a bath house, usually outside the walls of the fort
- workshops around the walls
- milecastles between the forts.

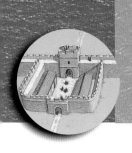

Roads

Roads were very important to the army. They could move soldiers and supplies around more easily with paved, well-drained roads. Roads were built higher in the middle and sloped to drains on either side, which took away the water that ran off the road. Using these roads, messengers could take orders from Rome to all parts of the **empire**. They could cover about 240 kilometres (150 miles) a day.

Ordinary people also used Roman roads. Traders carried all kinds of goods from one part of the empire to another. Places to eat and sleep were built along the busiest roads.

Soldiers built the roads, using local workers for digging and carrying. First, workers dug a trench about 1.8 metres deep. They flattened the earth at the bottom, adding a layer of sand. They placed big stones on top of this, holding them together with **cement**. Next they placed a layer of smaller stones and cement, then gravel, then sand and cement. Last, they put on a top layer of big, flat stones.

ROAD WORKS

Roman roads were very well made. The engineers changed how deep the layers were depending on how soggy the soil was. Some Roman roads still exist today, although most have been built over.

Engineers marked a route for the road. Workers pounded down each layer with a heavy stone on a pole while the cement was still wet. This made the road hard-wearing.

Work

Roman soldiers were sent to **forts** like those on Hadrian's Wall for years at a time. They spent very little time fighting, but they did drill exercises, practising fighting moves, every day. Because Roman soldiers fought as a group, they had to be able to move their spears, swords and shields at exactly the same time, to stop them getting tangled up. The soldiers also spent time keeping their weapons and armour in good condition.

The army thought it was important that soldiers always looked smart. They had to polish their helmets until they shone. They had special helmets like this one to wear for such events as a visit by the **emperor**.

As well as building roads, forts and walls, soldiers had long lists of duties. These changed around so, apart from training, they did different things each week. They checked everyone who wanted to go from one side of the wall to the other. They went out on **patrols,** exploring the enemy side of the wall. Some of the soldiers helped the local workers who made and mended the armour and equipment.

DRILL PRACTICE

In about AD 75, the Roman writer Josephus wrote about drill and training in the army: 'Every soldier practises daily, as if it were wartime. This means they can put up with the exhaustion and chaos of battle. They always beat armies that are less well trained.'

The army mostly bought its food from the local people. If people refused to sell them food, the soldiers simply took what they needed. Each soldier carried a sickle to cut **grain** – as shown in this carving – which was ground into flour for bread.

Clothes and armour

Soldiers wore linen underwear with a red **tunic** on top. In colder places, they also wore trousers to just below the knee. Their boots had nails on the bottom to give a good grip in mud or on slippery grass. Soldiers wore a helmet and armour to protect their shoulders and upper body – the parts most likely to get hit in battle.

INJURY POINTS

Armour was made out of strips of metal in layers, so the soldiers could move more easily. However, forearms and legs were unprotected and often injured.

Swords, like these gladii, needed to be kept sharp. Water troughs all over the **empire** have grooves in the stone surrounds, where soldiers pressed down on the stone again and again to sharpen their swords and daggers.

Pilum, or spear

Body armour

Helmet

Pole

Gladius, or sword

Pickaxe

Basket

Shield

A Roman soldier's equipment weighed about 35 kilograms. He had to carry or wear it while marching. He had:

- a long spear, called a pilum, for stabbing and throwing
- a sword, called a gladius, for stabbing
- a shield with a different pattern on for each **cohort**
- body armour and a helmet
- up to four long poles, to make a camp for the night
- a basket to carry a cooking pot
- a tin plate
- a small grindstone (to grind corn to flour), a sickle to cut corn, a saw and a pickaxe.

Health and hygiene

The Romans wanted a healthy army. Sick soldiers cannot fight. Because soldiers lived crowded together in **barracks**, any illness spread very quickly. The Romans knew that dirt could cause disease. So soldiers were expected to keep very clean. They had to wash themselves and their clothes regularly. Every **fort** had toilets and bath houses.

These Roman toilets show the stone seats and a drain at ground level. The drain had clean water running in it, so people could rinse the sponges they used as toilet paper.

TOILETS

The toilet was a large room with wooden seats around the sides. In the middle was a big basin of water for hand washing. Sponges on sticks were used as toilet paper, washed and re-used. They were rinsed in a small drain.

Each century had a doctor in charge of medical care. The doctor had several less well-trained helpers. These worked as nurses, cleaning and bandaging wounds and giving patients medicines. Doctors also treated day-to-day problems, such as boils, sore teeth, burns and eye infections. They used herbs to make medicines and ointments.

These surgeon's tools were found at Corbridge Fort on Hadrian's Wall. They were used for small operations, such as clearing out boils.

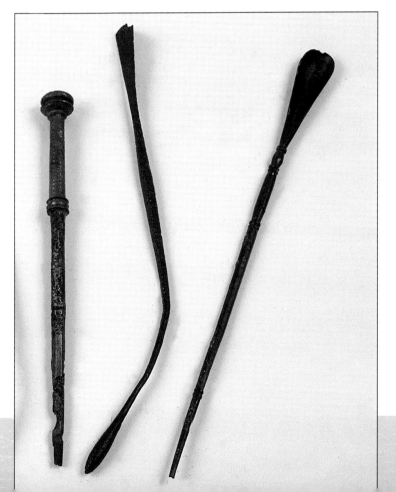

Barracks

When soldiers were on the move, they slept in tents, eight in each tent. In **forts** they lived in **barracks**, which had room for up to 100 soldiers. Barracks were long buildings divided up to give each 'tent' their own area of about 6.8 metres by 3.6 metres. This area had two rooms, one for sleeping in and one for the soldiers' equipment.

These barracks at Housesteads Fort on Hadrian's Wall were built as long buildings, one to each **cohort**. In about AD 300 they were rebuilt as eight separate blocks, with small lanes between them.

Barracks had only the most basic furniture. The army did not want soldiers to be too comfortable, or to spend too long in barracks. However, the army wanted healthy soldiers, so barracks were well built and did not leak or have draughts. Many barracks had fireplaces, to keep the soldiers warm and dry. A covered porch ran along one side, to give some covered outside space.

NO PRIVACY

The **centurion** had his own room at one end of the barracks. But ordinary soldiers had no privacy at all. They lived together and ate together. The army wanted them to think of themselves as part of a team all the time.

Barracks only had small windows, so they would often have been dark. Lamps like these, filled with oil, were burned for light, but they only gave a dim light, and often smoked badly.

Family life

Only the **praetor** in charge of the **fort**, who had his own house, was allowed to have his family living with him. The praetor's wife led a lonely life, with only her **slaves** for female company in the fort. **Officers'** families sometimes followed them and lived in nearby towns. These officers had to get permission to visit their families in their time off.

Sulpicia and her husband Ceralis had children while they were living at Vindolanda Fort. This child's shoe was found in their house.

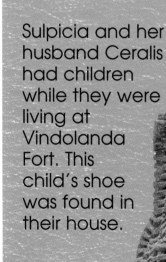

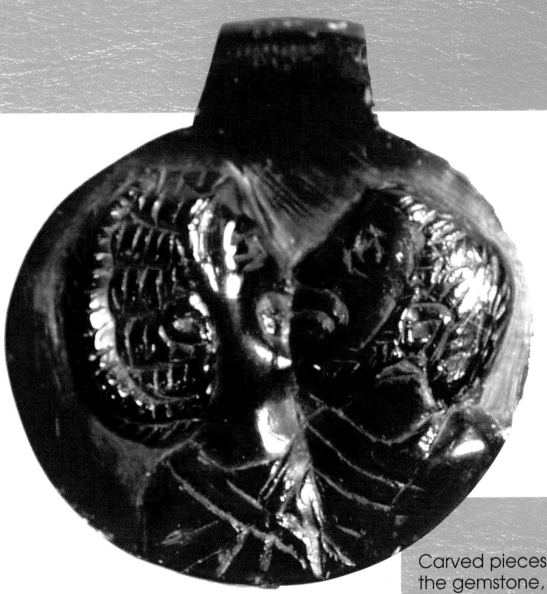

Ordinary soldiers had to leave their families behind when they joined the army. They were expected to live and work as a group, with the army as their 'family'. Sometimes soldiers married local women, or their families moved to be near them. Even so, the soldiers could only visit them with special permission from the praetor.

Carved pieces of the gemstone, jet, like this one, were often given when two people agreed to marry. Despite army disapproval, soldiers did marry and have families.

Off-duty activities

Soldiers did get some time off. They had to get permission to leave the **fort,** and had to be back by a set time. If a fort was a long way from a town, a small town grew up around it. Local people set up shops selling food and drink, pottery and cooking pots. There were workshops that made and repaired shoes and clothes.

In the ruins of the village outside Housesteads Fort, you can still see the groove that the big shutter at the front of this shop slid down into when the shop was shut up for the night.

The **praetor** and his **officers** visited each other and hired entertainers, such as dancers and acrobats, for parties. Ordinary soldiers who had families usually visited them when they had time off. Others went to inns or to the army bath house. In both these places they could gossip, eat, drink and gamble.

This gameboard and dice were found at Vindolanda Fort. The dice have been loaded – weights were put inside to make the numbers 1 and 6 come up most often.

Religion

The Romans worshipped many different gods and goddesses, who they believed controlled everyday life. So it was important to pray to the gods to keep them happy. Each **fort** had a room in the headquarters building that contained a **shrine** to the gods. There were also shrines and **temples** to the gods in the town outside the fort. Local gods were often worshipped here, too.

This altar to Mars, the god of war, was set up in Housesteads Fort. Mars was an important god to soldiers, who wanted him on their side in battle.

Many soldiers worshipped the god Mithras as a god of victory. Mithras was a sun god. He was worshipped secretly, unlike most Roman gods and goddesses. This means we do not know a lot about how soldiers worshipped Mithras, although we know he was important. We do not even know why Mithras was regarded differently.

MITHRAS

There was a *mithraeum,* a temple to Mithras, at Housesteads Fort on Hadrian's Wall. An altar to Mithras was found there, put up by a soldier called Litorius Pacatianus. People often promised the gods to put up an altar if the gods helped them.

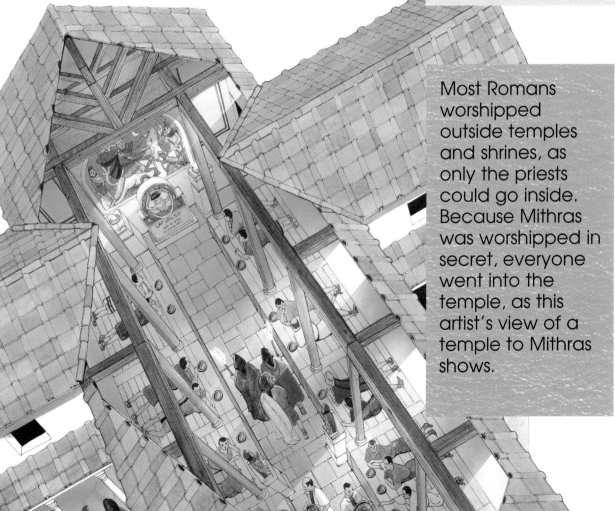

Most Romans worshipped outside temples and shrines, as only the priests could go inside. Because Mithras was worshipped in secret, everyone went into the temple, as this artist's view of a temple to Mithras shows.

Food

The Romans knew that eating properly helped people to keep healthy. So soldiers were fed healthy food. They ate three meals a day together. They had bread, porridge, cheese and plenty of fresh fruit and vegetables. They ate meat only occasionally. This was mostly from animals they hunted, such as rabbits or wild pigs. They mostly drank wine, unless there was clean, fresh water.

In forts like Vindolanda, **grain** was ground for flour on large stone querns. This is the bottom stone. Another stone was fixed on top of it and turned with a handle to grind the grain.

Roman recipe – army porridge

Roman soldiers used different sorts of **grains** to make their porridge. You can make a mix like their porridge using oatbran or, if you cannot find this, pinhead (very fine) oatmeal. Do not use oatflakes or ready prepared porridge oats. The quantities feed about four people.

WARNING: Do not cook anything unless there is an adult to help you.

1 Rub the bottom of the saucepan with a few drops of oil. Make sure to get into the edges.

2 Stir the oatbran or oatmeal and water together in a saucepan. Stir until it makes a thick mush.

3 Heat the saucepan gently – do not boil. At first, you do not have to stir all the time.

4 As the water gets hot, the oats will slowly swell up to make the mixture thicker.

5 Keep stirring until the mixture is as thick as a thick milkshake or a smoothie. It will take from 10 to 25 minutes of stirring.

Roman forts today

When the Romans left a country they had taken over, their **forts** and walls were often reused by the local people. They moved into the forts to defend themselves against other groups of people. When the Roman buildings were no longer needed for defence, the stone from them was used for new buildings. Today, remains of Roman forts are still being uncovered when places are dug up to build new offices, shops or homes.

REUSE OF STONES

To make their forts and walls, the Roman had dug stones out of the ground and shaped them. So reusing the stones saved local builders much work.

Not all the stones from forts and walls were taken away. Enough was left to work out what the buildings had been. Now places like Housesteads Fort in Britain are visited each year by thousands of people.

Glossary

archaeologist person who uncovers old buildings and burial sites to find out about the past

barracks building in a fort in which soldiers live

cement mixture of lime, water and powdered stone mixed together, which sets hard and binds together brick and stone

centurion officer in charge of a century – about 80 soldiers and 20 workers, in the Roman army

cohort group of about 480 soldiers and 120 workers

empire a country and all the other lands it controls

engineer person who knows how to build roads, buildings and bridges so that they are safe and can take heavy loads

fort place built to keep people, usually soldiers, safe from attack

grain fat seeds of some grasses that can be eaten. Barley, wheat, rice, oats and rye are all grains.

laws rules made by the people running a country

legion group of about 4800 soldiers and 1200 workers

officer person in the army who is in charge of ordinary soldiers

patrol group of soldiers that leave a fort and go around the local area, making sure there is nothing going on that could threaten the lives of Romans or the fort

praetor person in charge of a fort

records written lists and letters that show how something is run

shrine place where people come to pray to gods and goddesses and leave them gifts

slaves people who are bought and sold like property. They cannot leave their owners without permission.

stores all the things an army needs to keep it going, from tools to food and medicine

temple place where people pray to gods and goddesses

tunic T-shirt shaped piece of clothing that comes down to about the knees. Roman men, women and children all wore tunics.

More books to read

History of Britain: Roman Conquest of Britain, Brenda Williams (Heinemann Library, 1996)

See Through History: Ancient Rome, Simon James (Heinemann Library, 1996)

See Through History: Forts and Castles, Brian Williams (Heinemann Library, 1994)

The Life and World of Julius Caesar, Struan Reid (Heinemann Library, 2002)

Index